Design and Make

Fabric and Thread Collages

Jan Arundell and John Wright

J M Dent & Sons Ltd London

Filmset by BAS Printers Limited, Wallop,
Hampshire.
for J. M. DENT & SONS LTD
Aldine House . Albemarle Street . London

ISBN 0 460 04125 8

The authors would like to thank all
those people who contributed
photographs of their work and those
who gave permission for the inclusion
of work in their possession, in
particular Rev. Canon Parks,
M. A. Mosesson, Bryonny Caddick,
Pip Wright and Pat Philpott.

Grateful thanks go to Sheila Brown,
who assisted with the embroidery
samplers, to Annie Whitaker, for her
patience when correcting and typing
the manuscript, and to Chris Coburn,
for advice and assistance with some
of the photography.

The help and advice given by
Twilleys of Stamford and J. P. Coats
Ltd. is also gratefully acknowledged.

All samplers and collages in this book
are the work of John Wright, unless
otherwise stated, and the diagrams
were drawn by Jan Arundell.

Contents

1 *Victorian sampler produced by an eleven-year-old girl. This is typical of the samplers worked by young ladies of the period*

Introduction

Throughout his long career, man has taken great pride in decorating the objects which concern him intimately. He has paid particular attention to the clothes he wears and he has evolved elaborate ways of embellishing the fabrics from which they are made.

Even during periods when ornamentation is unfashionable, or is considered an unnecessary expense, fabrics continue to be decorated with imaginative weaving, printing and embroidery.

This unabated activity has led to the development of many interesting ways of using fabric, not the least of which is the art of fabric collage.

This is truly an art in the sense that it does not serve our workaday needs. Thus collages do not have to withstand the rigours of frequent washing and ironing, nor do they have to stand up to the hard wear to which more functional items are subjected. We are at liberty to concentrate our efforts on work that satisfies us because it looks attractive, and in this we are aided by the abundance of gay prints, rich weaves and beautiful threads that are readily available.

American terms are given in square brackets where they differ from the British.

2 Basic equipment stored in a cutlery
box. This is a beginner's kit. In time you
will collect other items specific to your
requirements. A filing system for all your
equipment will make your work easier.
Cutlery boxes make good filing trays

Basic Equipment

Hardware

To use the techniques described in this book, you will need the equipment in the following list. As you become proficient and acquire additional items, you will need to organize your bits and pieces. One way of doing this is to arrange them in cutlery trays.

a *Needles*. Keep a wide variety — they will all be needed for sewing with a full range of threads. Stored on a pin-cushion, they are readily available for quick selection.

b *Scissors*, both large and small. Very small pointed ones are useful for cutting detailed shapes from material. It is essential that all scissors are very sharp. A non-fray, decorative edge can be cut with pinking shears. Do not use your scissors for cutting paper or they will become blunt.

c *Long dressmaker's pins*, for holding bits and pieces in place whilst sewing.

d *Tailor's chalk*, for marking.

e *Tweezers/sharpened wax crayon*, for picking up small beads, sequins etc.

f *Thimble*. Some people do not find this necessary but it is useful when sewing tough material.

g *Embroidery hoop*. When work is not set up on a permanent frame or mount, it may be necessary to keep work areas stretched in a small embroidery hoop.
This enables the worker to control stitch tension. The best kind of embroidery hoop has a screw to tighten the outer ring.

Software

When designing with fabric there is a lot to take into consideration. The colour, texture, pattern and whether the surface is shiny or dull are all equally important. Certain patterned and textured fabrics have strong directional qualities and can be very dominant in a composition. Patterned fabrics can be muted by dipping them in a bath of dye. Work to the dye manufacturer's instructions and make sure the dye is the correct type for the material.

Whatever the colour or texture of the fabric you choose, its appearance will be strongly affected by the surrounding materials. Experiment by cutting out a number of squares 2×2 cm (about $\frac{3}{4} \times \frac{3}{4}$ in) from a piece of plain, coloured fabric and place them on as many different materials as possible. Stand away from the assemblage and try to assess the results. The squares will appear to vary in strength and colour depending on the background.

Repeat the exercise with squares of other colours and qualities.

a *Fabrics*. A visit to a large store will give some indication of the range available. Before purchasing any fabrics, it is advisable to become familiar with as many types as possible. Fabrics can be subdivided into :

i Plain surfaced, eg plain and satin weaves in cotton, rayon, Terylene, nylon, silk, wool etc. Other plain materials such as p.v.c., leather, felt etc., are equally suitable.

ii Textured, eg wools, including hand knitteds, jersey and tweeds. Coarse cottons such as canvas, binker, corduroy, cambric and hopsack. Hessian [burlap], towelling [terrycloth], rough linen, bouclé, mohair etc. Open structures such as nets, laces and open weave curtaining.

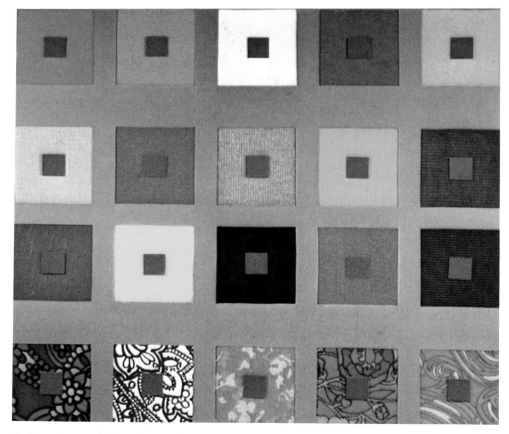

3 *Experiments with colour and texture*

b *Threads*. Fabrics can be cut up to make all manner of shapes, but threads have a natural linear quality which is useful to exploit. Even when they are sewn in elaborate stitches, such as raised chain band, the appearance is still linear.

i Plain threads include sewing cotton, embroidery cotton, knitting and crochet cotton, string, knitting wool, cord, tapestry wool, thrums (carpet thread offcuts) etc.

ii Threads with a sheen. Embroidery silk, thicker mercerized cotton, sisal string (can be dyed), raffia (not usually colour fast), shiny imitation raffias, metal threads etc.

iii Threads with a strong texture. Both wools and cottons can be obtained with lumps, slubs [twists], loops etc., and on page 39 you will find instructions for making your own textured thread.

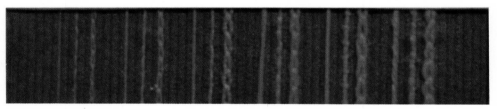

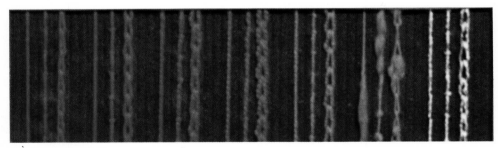

4 *Embroidery threads*

The threads on the top row are Coats/ Anchor products: a *Machine twist; sewing cotton;* b *Coton à broder;* c *Pearl cotton;* d *Stranded cotton;* e *Soft embroidery;* f *Tapisserie wool*

The threads on the bottom row are Twilleys products: a *Lysbet super cotton;* b *Crysette super No. 3 cotton;* c *Stalite No. 3 cotton;* d *Cortina crochet wool;* e *Lyscordet No. 3 cotton;* f *Bubbly slubbed cotton;* g *Gold fingering (metallic knitting or crochet thread)*

9

iv Other useful linear materials are braids, laces, shoe laces (available in many colours), fancy wrapping strings and ribbons etc. Most of these items can be split or dissected to make a finer thread if required.

Use a needle with an eye through which the thread will pass easily, but not too loosely. If the eye is too small, it is difficult to pull the thread through the fabric and in so doing, the fabric could become distorted or stretched. If the eye of the needle is too large, it is likely to come unthreaded.

Thick and/or heavily textured threads cannot be pulled through certain fabrics. These can be anchored to the right side of the work by couching (p. 17).

Adhesives
Adhesives can be used as an alternative to stitches for fastening the basic shapes of the design to the background. It is the easiest method for young children who could find traditional methods of appliqué too time consuming.

Fixing with adhesive is quick and positive. Once the fabric is fixed in position it is difficult to move.

Always apply adhesives thinly with a spreader (a small rectangular piece of cardboard or thin plastic such as the end of a ruler). Use a very light touch to prevent the adhesive penetrating to the right side of the fabric where it could cause a stain.

Adhesive causes the fabric to lose its elasticity. This could present problems if the work requires stretching later (see pp. 55–58).

Fabrics to which adhesive has been applied become stiff, thicker and more difficult to sew through.

All adhesives, even transparent ones, stain thin fabrics.

a *Milliner's Glue* [a thick rubber cement] is of such consistency that it is unlikely to penetrate thick fabrics. It can be rubbed off fingers and shiny surfaces.

b *Cow Gum* [rubber cement] is thinner but with similar rubbery qualities which enable it to be cleaned off fingers and tables. It makes the fabric more rigid and has a limited life.

c *Marvin Medium* [white glue] is a PVA based adhesive which will stick most materials except some metals and plastics. Before drying, it is soluble in water and can be washed from clothes, but it is difficult to remove when set.

There are other suitable adhesives. Check the manufacturer's instructions before use and test the adhesives on a scrap of the fabric. Never use an adhesive of thin consistency as it will penetrate the fabric too easily.

Method of Working

Selecting a subject

Even though you may possess a knowledge of embroidery stitches, you could still feel overwhelmed when confronted with a large pile of fabrics, threads, buttons, sequins and ribbons of many colours. If all the available items were included in one collage, the result could be somewhat chaotic. So at the beginning it is best to restrict yourself to a simple theme and as you grow confident develop your ideas in whichever direction promises to give the best results.

Here are some themes which could help you with your first attempt.

a Experiment with one stitch and see how many textures you can achieve.

b Make a design using only straight or curved lines.

c Limit yourself to tones of one colour and see how many rich effects you can make by varying *i* the fabrics used ; *ii* the yarns and stitches used.

d Experiment with stitches sewn in concentric circles.

Choose a subject from this list, or decide on one of your own choice, assemble all your equipment and you are ready to start the collage.

Selecting a background fabric

Choose one that is sufficiently robust to carry all the extra fabrics and stitching that will be applied to it. It should be firm and not stretch too much in any one direction. Test it to see that a needle and thread can be pulled through without leaving a hole or mark, so that if at any stage you change your mind, it will not be possible to detect where stitches have been unpicked.

Materials suitable as background fabrics are loosely woven linens, closely woven wools, bouclé, Hessian [burlap], short piled cotton towelling [terrycloth] etc.

Holding the background fabric during working

Some people like to hold the fabric loosely in the hands at all stages, but beginners may find that this results in some of the sewing being incorrectly tensioned, causing a puckered effect. This can be overcome if the fabric is held firmly in a traditional embroidery hoop which is moved around as required. However, this kind of frame tends to crush pile fabrics, leaving a permanent mark. An alternative method is to use drawing-pins [thumb tacks] to fasten the fabric to the frame which is to hold it permanently when the work is finished. If the tension works slack, the drawing-pins can be adjusted and the work finally stretched when it is complete (see pp. 55–58).

Selecting the fabrics to be applied to the background

Keep a varied, comprehensive collection of fabrics. Experiment with colours, textures and patterns by cutting out shapes and placing them on the background in various positions and combinations (fig 3). Note that certain fabrics, eg corduroys and knitteds, have two very dissimilar sides. Try them both. Thin materials which are likely to fray can be made more substantial by using iron-on interfacing before cutting. This will not cloud the fabric and it is not expensive. It also enables you to cut intricate shapes from delicate fabrics. When you have finally decided on a satisfactory arrangement, the fabrics can be fixed to the background with stitches or adhesive.

Selecting the threads

Always have a large collection to hand, for it is difficult to decide beforehand what you are likely to need. Try out as many threads as you can, pinning them in place, until you have a satisfactory arrangement. Bear in mind that the threads you apply can substantially alter the appearance of your work.

If you need to mark out the fabric prior to sewing, use tailor's chalk. Then sew a tacking [basting] thread along the line and rub off the chalk before embroidering, as it is difficult to remove the chalk from beneath heavy stitching.

NB It is all too easy to become so engrossed in your work that a distant and objective view is seldom taken. It is difficult to assess a design at close range, so from time to time stand well away from the work — at least two metres [about two yards] — and try to evaluate it as a whole.

Three Basic Stitches (1)

We have selected three basic stitches. They are simple to learn and can be used to produce some extraordinarily rich effects. Try out the stitches with threads of varying thicknesses and colours. You may be surprised how versatile each one can be. Then combine them to make a complete collage.

NB All diagrams are designed for use by right-handed people. Those who are left-handed may find it useful to hold a mirror at 90° to the diagram, along the side of the stitch, and read the mirror image.

Embroidery has been practised for so long that a most bewildering array of stitches has been developed. The beginner may encounter difficulty in deciding which stitch to use. Some are so complicated that it takes quite a time to master them.

Running and back stitch
Running stitch is the simplest continuous stitch. Used conventionally it makes a broken line of straight, even stitches. Back stitch is only a slight variation on this and forms a continuous line of straight stitches.

5a *Running stitch;* b *Back stitch*

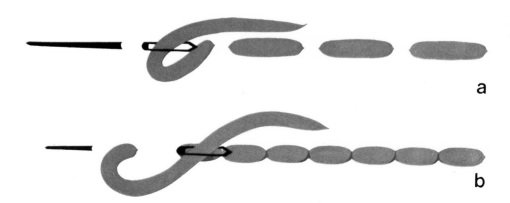

a

b

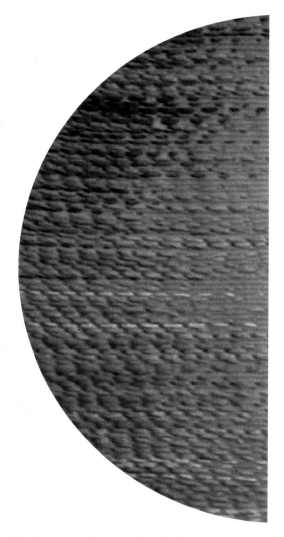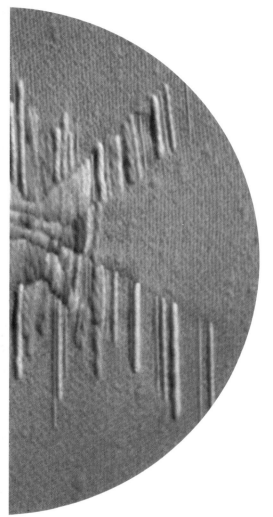

6a *Running stitch and back stitch* 6b *Single stitches*

14

7 *Sampler showing running and straight stitches used to make regular and irregular patterns*

Things to do

a Learn how to make rows of evenly spaced running and back stitches and then try varying the lengths of the stitches.

b Work two rows of running stitch, one on top of the other, alternating the positions of the stitches.

c Work the same exercise in two colours and/or two thicknesses of thread.

d Running stitch is particularly adaptable. Practise some of the regular patterns shown in fig. 7. Make up some of your own and then see if you can invent some irregular ones.

8 'Pink Chicken'. A collage made up
almost entirely from straight stitches

16

Three Basic Stitches (2)

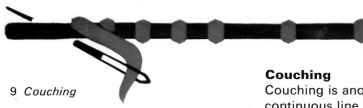

9 *Couching*

10a *Couching in straight lines*
10b *Couching in curves*

Couching

Couching is another way of making a continuous line and is particularly useful for making smooth flowing curves of any radius. Couching is the most common and the simplest way of fastening down threads which are too thick to penetrate the background fabric. The ends of such threads should be bound with a fine, self-coloured yarn to prevent fraying.

Things to do

a Couch down a thick thread with a fine one, then vice versa.

b Vary the spaces between the couching stitches.

c Experiment with contrasting couching and couched thread colours.

Each of these will result in a different effect.

Three Basic Stitches (3)

a

Chain stitch

This is a simple stitch with which you can create a textured line. The proportions between the width and length of the stitch can be altered to vary the appearance. Because of its bulk, chain stitch is useful for filling in areas and making textured surfaces.

11a *Chain stitch*
11b *Chain stitch (opened out)*

b

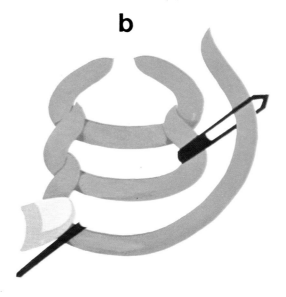

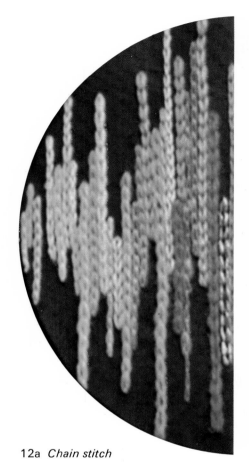
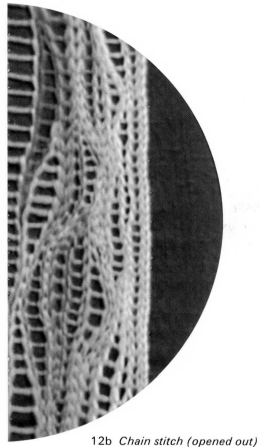

12a *Chain stitch*   12b *Chain stitch (opened out)*

Things to do

a Learn how to use the stitch and
  how to control the proportions so
  that you can make various ladder
  effects.

b See how many kinds of area
  filling you can evolve.

c Use a chain stitch to hold down
  another thread. This is similar to
  couching.

13 *Detail of 'Sunset'. Pieces of fabric held down with running stitch, couching and chain stitch.*

14 *Vegetable designs by ten-year-old girls and boys.*
Running, couching and chain stitches are used.

21

Further Stitches

Herringbone stitch

This stitch makes a criss-cross line. Two or more rows worked closely make a good filling or texture.

The stitch is worked horizontally from left to right. The beginner would be advised to use two tacking threads to mark the top and bottom of the row of stitches if he requires an even result.

15 *Herringbone stitch. The diagram shows the two needle positions*

Things to do

a Having mastered the stitch as above, try doubling it by working another row of stitches in the spaces, making diamond shapes.

b Work a row of herringbone stitches between two lines of tacking thread which are not parallel.

c Vary the density of the row by working stitches closely together and widely spaced.

16a *Herringbone stitch*

16b *Herringbone stitch worked between two lines which are not parallel*

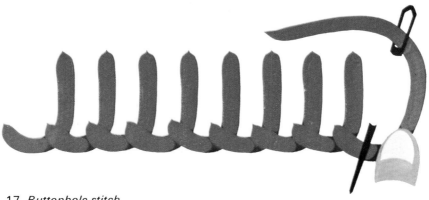

17 *Buttonhole stitch*

Buttonhole stitch

This is a stitch which produces a heavy line with feathering on one side. Apart from being very decorative it is a most functional stitch. If worked compactly, it can be used to appliqué a material to a background, particularly if the former is prone to fraying. It is a useful edging stitch for cut work. When worked really closely it makes a tough buttonhole.

Work the stitch from left to right. If you cannot keep it regular, mark the intended depth of stitch with two rows of tacking threads which can be removed when the stitching is complete.

Things to do

a Practise making a neat, even row of buttonhole stitches.

b Vary the spacing of the stitches so that you produce a line which is more and less compact.

c Vary the length of the feathering along a row of stitches.

d Sew a row of buttonhole stitches over a thick thread to make a bulky line.

e Sew one row of buttonhole stitches, turn the work round and sew another row so that the two feathered edges alternate.

f Make areas of filling from both compact and widely spaced stitches.

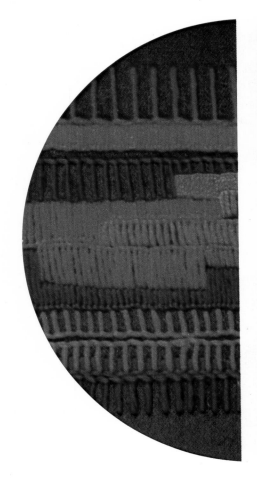

18a *Buttonhole stitch*

18b *Buttonhole stitch worked in uneven ways*

Feather and cretan stitches

These stitches are a development of the buttonhole, giving a feathered effect on both sides of a zig-zag line. Feather stitch is light and open, cretan is exactly the same but worked in wide, shallower proportions, giving a much heavier line. It is sometimes used as a filling for small shapes, the edge of the stitch following the edge of the shape to be filled.

The stitch is worked from top to bottom. The needle is drawn through the material at an angle from right to left as in fig 19. This is alternated under the left-hand side of the stitch where the needle is drawn through the fabric from left to right. Each time, the needle must be pulled over the thread which is held down with the thumb.

b

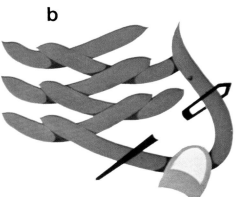

19a *Feather stitch*
19b *Cretan stitch*

20a *Cretan and feather stitch*

20b *Cretan and feather stitch worked in uneven ways*

Things to do

a Try varying the shape of the stitch.

b Make fillings for small oval, circular, rectangular and triangular shapes.

Raised chain band

This is used as a filling stitch that is worked on a previously sewn 'ladder' rather than through the fabric. It makes a richly textured surface which can be in one or two colours.

First sew the ladders — wide enough to take the required number of rows of chain band. Then weave the chain band, working towards yourself on the horizontal rungs of the ladder. Take the needle under each rung, up to the left and down to the right.

Things to do

a Work on self-coloured ladders and ladders of contrasting colour.

b Vary the thickness of the threads with which you make the ladder and with which you sew the chain.

c Vary the distance between the rungs of the ladders.

21 *Raised chain band*

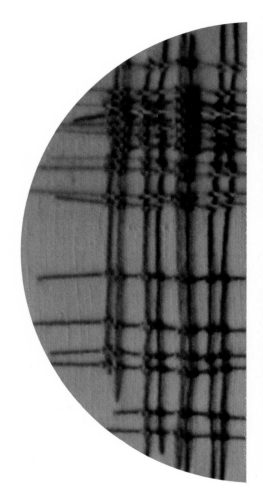

22a *Raised chain band worked on very long ladders*

22b *Raised chain band worked upon itself*
(i) Left hand side worked in order of numbering
(ii) Right hand side shows a closer worked area

23 *Further work on ladders*

Further stitches on ladders

Unless you keep this work in a frame at all stages, you may have difficulties with the tension of the stitches.

The 'ladders' are made up of strands of thread which float freely over the surface of the material. They are attached only at each end. If the thread is too bulky to penetrate the background fabric, bind the ends to prevent fraying and stitch down with a fine matching thread.

As soon as you have stitched a framework of floating parallel ladder rungs, you can begin the decorative work. Thread the needle under and over the rungs in any order you wish, without sewing through the fabric except where you start and finish the row. The ends of the stitches are best concealed under a rung. This sewing technique is similar to weaving.

The diagrams and samplers show some simple repeating patterns.

Things to do

a Having mastered the technique, experiment with 'weaving' a variety of threads. As the stitching does not pass through the fabric, it is possible to work with quite heavily textured threads.

b Try working on background threads that are *i* unevenly spaced; *ii* not parallel.

c Work out some designs which do not repeat evenly down the length of the ladder.

24 *Further work on ladders*

Twisted chain stitch

This stitch makes a knotted line. When the knots are small and the spaces between large, it is known as coral stitch. Traditionally it was used as a border stitch and to outline shapes.

Work from top to bottom in a similar manner to chain stitch but ensure that the needle enters the fabric outside the previous chain and to the left of the thread. The factors controlling the proportions of the stitch are *i* the distance between two chains; *ii* the place the needle enters the fabric; *iii* the amount of fabric taken up.

Things to do

a Try varying the distance between the chains. You will see from the samplers that the character of the stitch can vary tremendously.

b Experiment with criss-cross patterns, sewing chains of different colours crossing one another.

25 *Twisted chain stitch*

26a *Twisted chain stitch*

26b *Twisted chain stitch with varying lengths between each stitch*

Knotted cable stitch

This stitch makes a rich, chunky line. It is a little more difficult to master than some of the earlier stitches, but it is well worth the effort. If you have learnt how to sew a twisting chain stitch, you know how to make the first stage of this stitch.

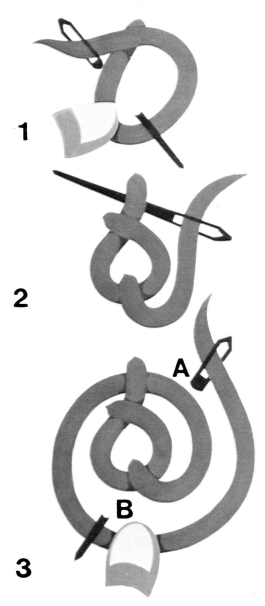

1 A Twisted Chain Stitch.

2 The needle is taken (right to left) round the back of the chain stitch and under the thread. Do not catch up any of the fabric.

3 The circular movement is continued right round the stitch and the needle is pushed through the fabric, underneath the stitch, A to B.

4 Repeat the process, commencing with a twisted chain stitch under the completed knotted cable stitch.

Things to do

a Practise the stitch until you can make an even chain.

b Try altering the shape of the stitch by taking more of the fabric onto the needle at stage 3 – in other words, increase the distance between points A and B.

27 *Knotted cable stitch*

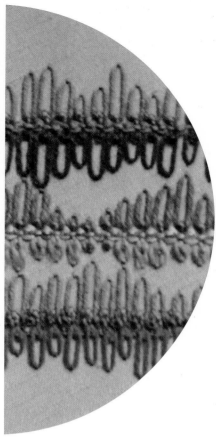

28a *Knotted cable stitch*

28b *Knotted cable stitch. The distance between A and B is lengthened as in fig 27 part 3*

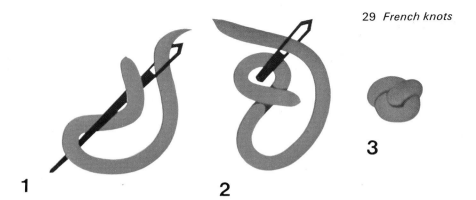

1   **2**   **3**

French knots

These are small neat dots which can be made singly, in a row, or grouped to form a textured surface.

Bring the thread through to the front of the fabric.

1 Hold the thread down with the left thumb and twist the tip of the needle round the thread two or three times.

2 Keeping the thumb firmly in place, draw the needle back and push it through the fabric near to the place where it emerged.

Bullion knots

These have similar uses to the french knot but are larger and more elongated in form.

1 Insert the needle as if to make a back stitch, allowing the point to come through the fabric at the place where the thread originally emerged (A).

2 Keep the needle in this position in the fabric and wrap the thread around it as many times as is necessary to make a knot wide enough to fill the stitch length.

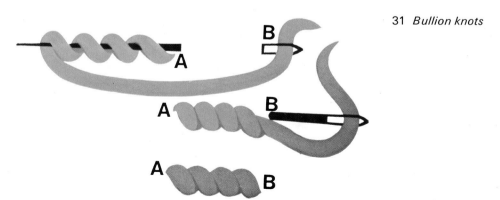

31 *Bullion knots*

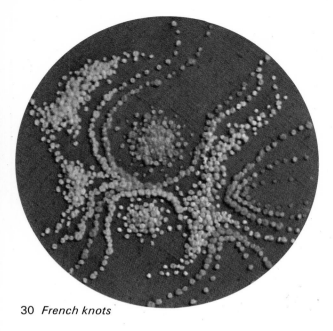

30 *French knots*

32 *Bullion knots*

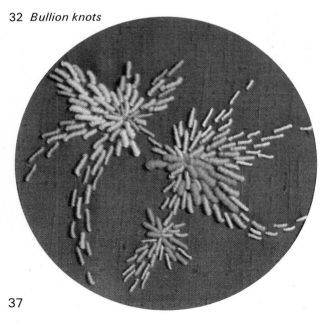

3 Holding the thumb on the coil of thread, pull the needle through and push it back into the fabric where it was previously inserted (B).

With care and practice, you will learn to make the stitch lie neatly, and be able to estimate the number of coils required to make a given length of stitch.

Things to do

a It may take a little time to make even stitches, so keep practising.

b If you should find the bullion knot too difficult to master, make loose bars of thread on the surface of the fabric and over sew them several times until you have achieved the same effect. Though rather time consuming, this is easier for young children than making the traditional bullion stitch.

c Make the distance between A and B small and increase the number of coils on the needle. This will result in raised and looped bullion knots.

37

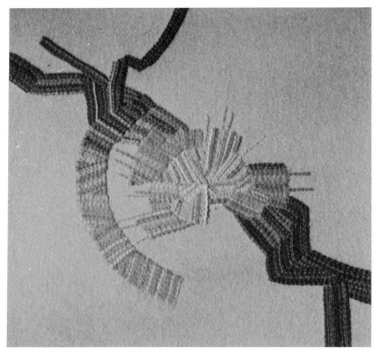

33 *'Shatter'*
shows most of
the stitches
described
previously. It is
worked on a
coarse wool
background.

34 *Detail from*
'New York'—
similar techniques
to those used in
fig 33 to create
a collage in a
more sophisti-
cated way.

Making Textured Threads

Although one can buy factory prepared textured threads, it is useful to be able to make a special thread to add the final touch to a design. The following techniques can be used to make varying thicknesses and qualities of thread.

Plaiting [Braiding]

Most people know how to make a three-strand plait [braid]. This method is easily extended to make a plait of any number of strands. The more strands used, the broader and flatter the plait will be.

Cords are made by twisting several threads together. Take a group of threads and fasten one end over a nail or hook. Twist the other end of the group until a tight rope is formed. Keep the rope taut with one hand and hold it exactly in the centre with the other. Still keeping the whole thing taut, bend the rope in two and when you release the hand which was in the centre, the two halves will spring together, making a neat cord of twice the thickness. When the cord is released from its support, bind the end to stop it fraying, and the cord will never untwist.

Knotting a single thread

An occasional knot tied in a thick thread can make an interesting feature.

Knotting two threads

Use two threads and keep tying one knot on top of another until a thicker, knobbly yarn is made. Use different knots to achieve various effects.

Bunching

Most knitting and sewing yarns are made up of a number of spun threads which have been doubled together in the factory by a process similar to cording. If the yarn is not too tightly twisted, you will be able to hold one of the component threads and slide the others along it, making bunches occur from time to time along the length of the yarn.

Buttonhole knotting

Two rows of buttonhole stitch (a right- and a left-hand version) can be knotted with the fingers around a taut central thread.

Crocheting

There are many crochet stitches which can be used to form a decorative thread.

Knitting

A textured thread can be made from a single long row of knitting or just two or three rows, using a variety of stitches. Alternatively, cast on two or three stitches and knit many rows, to the required length.

Most of these home-made threads
will be so lumpy that they must be
couched down to the surface of the
fabric rather than sewn through it.
Try these techniques with single
colours and combinations of colours
and with several thicknesses of
threads, and invent some methods of
your own.

35, 36 *Making textured threads:*
a *Plaiting;* b *Twisting threads together;*
c *Occasional knots in two threads;*
d *Knotting in one thread;* e *Two threads
knotted closely together;* f *Bunching*
g *Buttonhole knotting on itself;* h *Buttonhole knotting on a thinner cord;* i *Buttonhole knotting on two thinner cords;*
j *Crochet—one row of chain stitch;* k *A
knitted chain;* l *Two stitches knitted many
times;* m *Two examples of a cast-on row
and a cast-off row of knitting*

Fringing

Very exotic effects are obtained by using a variety of thread colours and lengths. Make strips of fringing by knotting pre-cut lengths of wool, etc. round two threads held taut, as in the diagram. The completed strips are couched into place on the collage.

37 *'Florid Yak'. A combination of fine embroidery and heavy fringing*

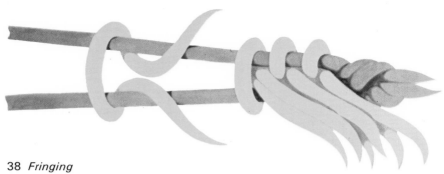

38 *Fringing*

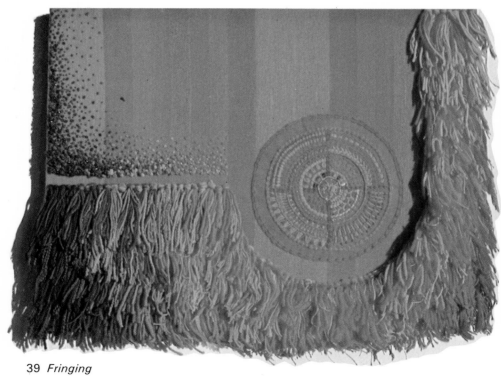

39 *Fringing*

Looping

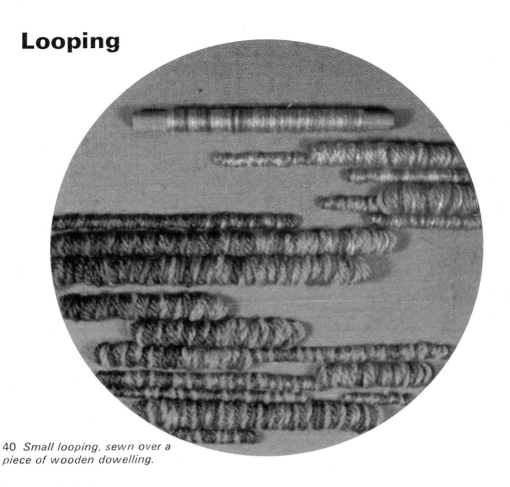

40 *Small looping, sewn over a piece of wooden dowelling.*

This is a useful technique for creating a bulky three dimensional effect. Worked compactly, with a variety of threads, it can give an unusually rich result.

1 Place a former [rod] in position on the material. The former can be a pencil, piece of card or curtain rod.

2 Sew over the former and through the material many times.

3 Remove the former by sliding it out of the row of stitches.

The size of the loop is determined by the width of the former. Curved rows of loops can be made by sewing over a flexible former such as a plastic coated curtain wire or plastic tubing.

Large looping made over a card (as in fig 41) will need small stitches at the base of the loops to prevent them pulling out.

The pink thread in fig 41 is used to hold a previous row of loops in place whilst the next row is worked. This is removed when the work is complete.

41 *Large looping, sewn over a card*

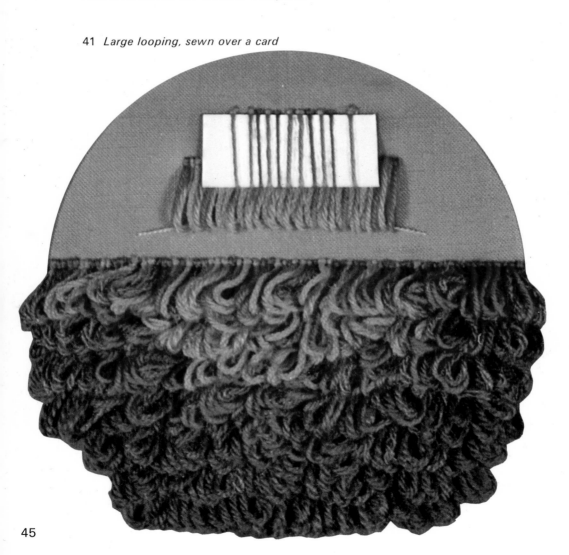

Raising Areas of Fabric

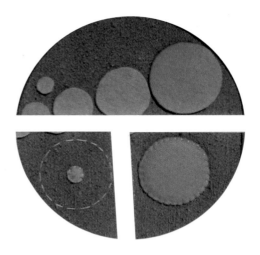

42 *The felt method of raising areas of fabric:* a *Stage 2;* b *Stage 3;* c *The Finished 'hill'*

This section shows how simple it is to make collages which are three dimensional, almost sculptural in quality.

Below are three techniques for raising areas of fabric. Each one produces a different effect and therefore has its particular application. Having read through the instructions and studied the illustrations, you will be able to decide which method, or combination of methods is most suitable for your work.

The felt method

1 Sew a tacking [basting] thread on the background to mark the shape of the area you wish to raise.

2 Cut out a series of felt shapes with which you will be able to build the 'hill'. The largest shape should be exactly the same as the shape marked on the background fabric, the rest should decrease in size, like a series of contour lines. The colour of the largest felt shape may be the same as the background or in contrast to it, depending on the desired effect.

3 When the series of shapes is complete, place the smallest one on the background, exactly in the centre of the tacked shape and oversew it neatly into place.

4 The second smallest shape is placed on top of the first one, again in the centre of the tacked shape, and oversewn into place.

5 The process is repeated with each larger shape in turn until all the pieces of felt are in place.

Making a collection

A visit to the haberdashery [notions or sewing supplies] department of a large store will give you some idea of the wealth of tiny beads, buttons and sequins available. Large wooden beads, like the ones on the sampler, are found in craft and educational shops. Seeds may be collected and dried. Some, such as pale coloured melon seeds, are easily dyed with coloured inks or textile dyes. Old jewelry can be dismantled to provide useful bits and pieces. You could ask your friends to save all broken necklaces and discarded buttons. When designing with these items, try them both sides up—the backs may be more interesting.

47 *Sampler showing a decorative use of hardware*

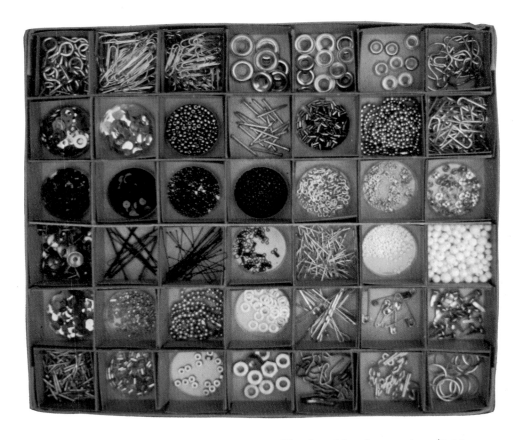

48 *Beads and various components filed
in a cardboard box*

The local hardware store is an
inexpensive and unconventional
source of small decorative items for
collage work. Look carefully at the
shape and detail of tiny washers,
nuts and screws. Little rust proof
nails are now made in many colours.
Cup hooks and spring washers can
be arranged in intricate geometric
patterns. Other items from haberdashery [notions] or stationery shops,

such as hairclips, paper clips, hooks and eyes and press studs [snaps] can all be used from time to time. The list is endless, so keep your eyes open and you will soon have a useful collection.

Keep your collection in an orderly fashion so that you can see what is available. Egg cartons, arranged in larger cardboard boxes or drawers, make excellent filing trays.

Designing with components

Work out your design by moving the components around on the background until you are satisfied with the arrangement. Tiny items, such as small beads or sequins, are most easily lifted with a pair of tweezers or picked up with a sharpened wax crayon or piece of candle. Very tiny beads may be easily managed if you put them on a thread first and couch this on to your work. You may need a thin beading needle.

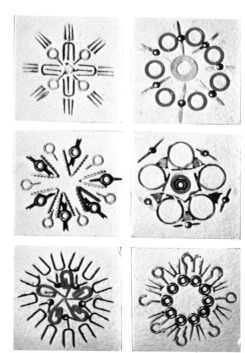

49 *Designs for embroidery by nine-year-old boys and girls. The components are glued onto card*

Stitching components

Unless you wish to make a feature of the stitches used to hold these items in place, a colourless nylon or 'invisible' thread is recommended for sewing as it will be virtually invisible on the final collage. It is more difficult to handle than ordinary sewing cotton and is not suitable for use by young children.

Silver or gold coloured items could be sewn down with silver or gold Lurex thread, but this is not very strong and would not support heavy items. Fine fuse wire could make an alternative thread.

Explore and experiment. You will find a great deal of pleasure in combining common objects to form exciting and unusual patterns.

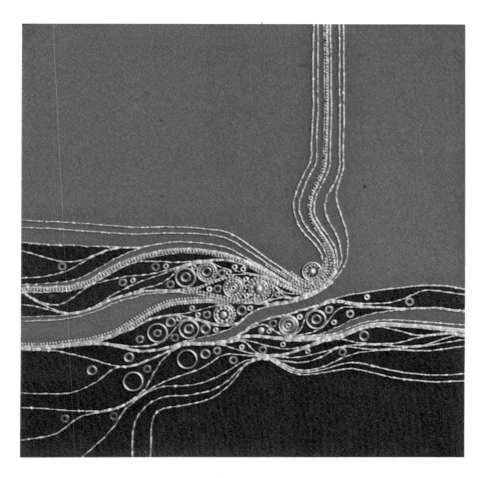

50 'Gold Flow'. The lines are metallic
knitting yarn, gold braid and brass chain,
couched into position with a transparent
nylon thread. The circular motifs include
curtain rings, washers, nuts and paper clips.

Mounting a Collage

A box frame is a valuable piece of equipment as it has a dual purpose. It will hold the collage whilst it is being worked and can provide permanent support when it is completed and finally stretched. Used as a permanent support, the box frame gives the finished collage a substantial appearance.

On the other hand, if you wish to put the finished collage inside a picture frame, it must be stretched over a thin board.

Making a box frame
Wood – planed deal about 2 × 3 cms [¾ × 1¼ ins]
Tenon saw [back saw]
Mitre block
4 cm [1½ ins] oval nails and hammer
Impact adhesive (Evo Stick etc) [contact cement]

1 Decide on the size of the frame required.

2 Mark out accurately four lengths of wood, one for each side of the frame.

3 Place each piece in a mitre block and cut away the surplus as shown by the red broken line in fig 51a.

4 Put a thin coat of adhesive on each of the cut edges and allow to dry. (This will seal the surface of the wood.)

5 Put a second thin coat of adhesive on each cut edge and allow it to dry for the time specified by the manufacturer.

6 Bring together the pieces of wood in exactly the correct position – once they touch they will stick fast.

7 Hammer the nails into the corners as in fig 51b. Take care to put them along the line of the wood grain so that they do not split the wood.

8 If the frame is large, you may need to add a centre piece to prevent the sides bending, but this could get in the way when you are sewing, so do not put it into position until just before the final stretching of the collage.

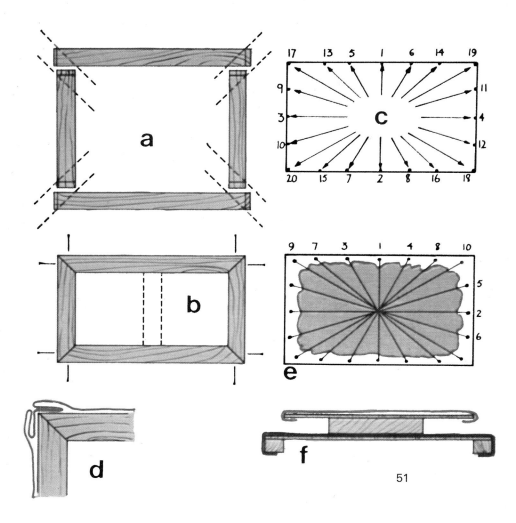

51

Stretching fabric over a box frame

Background fabric or finished collage
Drawing-pins [thumb tacks]
Tacks and hammer or staples and
staple gun
Box frame

At whatever stage you stretch the
work, you should find these notes
helpful.

1 The fabric to be stretched should be several centimetres [2 or 3 ins] larger than the outside dimensions of the box frame.

2 Work in the order shown in fig. 51c, pulling the fabric from the centre to the edges and corners of the frame and fastening it provisionally with drawing-pins on the back of the frame.

3 When the drawing-pins are in position, check the fabric by patting it all over with the flat of the hand to locate any irregularities in the tension.

4 After you have made any necessary adjustments, fix the fabric permanently into position with tacks or staples.

Pleating the fabric at the corners of a box frame

1 Fold the fabric to distribute the surplus evenly, as in fig 51d. Pin [tack] it in position.

2 Oversew the corner neatly.

Stretching fabric over hardboard [fiberboard]

Fabric or collage to be stretched
Piece of hardboard, smaller in size than above
Strong thread and needle for stretching
Backing material
Thread and needle for sewing backing material
Scissors.

As drawing-pins [thumb tacks] cannot be pushed into hardboard, it is not possible to stretch the fabric provisionally.

1 Place the finished collage face downwards on the work surface. Put the hardboard, smooth side downwards, symmetrically on top of it.

2 Fold the edges of the collage onto the back of the hardboard.

3 Hold the collage in place by sewing lines of thread very tightly, finishing off each one before starting on the next. Work in the order shown in fig 51e.

4 Put an extra thread between each one shown in the diagram.

5 Turn the work over at every stage to check the tension. If the correct tension is maintained, the collage will remain perfectly flat.

6 Sew the backing material in place. It should be 2 or 3 cms [about an inch] smaller than the hardboard. This will help to keep the tension even and tidy up the back of the work.

7 The finished work will now fit snugly into the rebate of a picture frame or it can be raise-mounted as described in the next section.

NB Hardboard is not suitable for holding fabric during sewing as the board prevents a needle being pushed right through the work.

Making a raised mount

1 Make a shallow box frame, slightly larger than the collage, as in fig 51a and b. Fit a piece of hardboard over the frame and glue it into position.

2 This is the background support for the collage and may be painted a suitable colour or covered in fabric.

3 Position a block or blocks of wood on the background in such a way that they will support the collage without being visible. Screw in place.

4 Use impact adhesive to fasten the collage to the supporting blocks. Be sure to align the collage correctly with the background before lowering it onto its supports, as once the components are placed together, it will be impossible to re-position them.

Stretching a puckered collage

Piece of softboard
[paper board]   ⎫ larger than
2 sheets blotting paper ⎭ collage
Dressmaking pins

No matter how careful you have been with your sewing, the finished work may be slightly puckered. The following technique should eliminate all except major wrinkles and can be used with all materials except those that would be spoilt by dampness.

1 Place the softboard on a flat surface and put the two sheets of dampened blotting paper on the top.

2 Put the finished collage, face side up, on top of the blotting paper and stretch and pin out in the same order as on the box frame. In order that the pins will function efficiently, put them into the board at a 45° angle, with the points towards the centre of the collage.

3 Leave the assemblage for one week or until it has completely dried out.

NB If the fabric is likely to fray, apply a strip of iron-on interfacing around the rear edge before applying the pins.

Cleaning
a Collage

52 *A hanging in
Stoneleigh Church,
Warwickshire*

A fabric collage that has been hanging unprotected for some time will become dusty. Do not attempt to clean it by washing or dry cleaning, but brush the surface gently with an old tooth brush, or vacuum it carefully, preferably with a small hand cleaner.

Small stains can be removed with one of the patent spot removers. Always test the product first on the reverse side of the collage to make sure it does not leave a stain on the material.

Although a collage can be kept clean by mounting it behind a sheet of glass, this is not recommended as the surface quality of the work will not be seen to advantage.

Introduction to Dress Embroidery

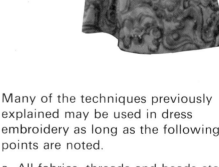

54 *Appliqué dress designed and made by Pip Wright, a third year student, Walsall College of Education. The skirt is of bonded jersey, appliquèd with* crêpe *and embroidered with hand-made corded threads.*

53 *Machine embroidered* crêpe *dress, designed and made by Pat Phillpott.*

Many of the techniques previously explained may be used in dress embroidery as long as the following points are noted.

a All fabrics, threads and beads etc should be tested for colour fastness and shrinkage before application.

b Avoid long stitches, as they are likely to catch and pull when worn, and cleaning processes may distort them.

Museums and Helpful Organizations

55 *Man's goatskin glove. The cuff is covered and lined with silk and embroidered with silver gilt thread and seed pearls. English, circa 1590. Photograph by courtesy of The Museum of Leathercraft, Walsall.*

Embroideries and fabric collages are to be found in museums, stately homes, churches and temples throughout the world. It is very interesting to explore your locality and find out what it has to offer. If you chat with people in museums, churches and even antique shops, you should quickly get an idea of the local scene and you will find out about other sources of information to help you with your enquiry.

Having investigated your local area, you could continue your enquiry on a national basis. Capital cities have large museums devoted entirely to the history of craftwork. Most countries have specialized in needlecraft at some period; e.g. Egypt, Greece, Persia, India, America and many central European countries are noted for their appliqué work. When you go on holiday, take a camera and note book and see what you can find out about the work produced in the places you visit. This kind of task gives real purpose to a holiday and you can come home feeling much rewarded for your effort.

Useful Addresses

American Crafts Council,
44 West 53rd Street, New York,
NY 10019.

The Council for Small Industries in Rural Areas,
35 Camp Road, Wimbledon Common,
London SW19 4UW.
Issues a small booklet of names and addresses of craftsmen all over the UK.

The Craft Centre,
Earlham Street, London WC2.
Exhibition hall and sale room for all crafts.

The Embroiderers Guild,
73 Wimpole Street,
London W1M 8AX and 30 East
60th Street, New York, NY 10022
and local branches in UK and USA.
The guild promotes interest in all aspects of the craft.

Local libraries will supply information on part-time courses in their area.

Suppliers

All the items used in this book are obtainable from good haberdashery [notions] shops or department stores. Two shops which carry a wide range of materials are:

The Needlewoman,
Regent Street, London.

John Lewis Ltd,
Oxford Street, London.

If you have difficulty, or wish to buy large quantities of materials, the following companies will help:

Britain
Beads
Ells & Farrier Ltd, 5 Princes Street, Hanover Square, London W1.

Canvas, single and double
Mrs. Joan L. Trichett,
110 Marsden Road, Burnley, Lancs.

Metal Threads
Toye, Kenning & Spencer Ltd,
Regalia House, Red Lion Square,
London WC1.

Milliner's Glue and Haberdashery
McCulloch & Wallis Ltd,
25 Dering Street, London W1.

Threads
J. & P. Coats Ltd,
155 St Vincent Street, Glasgow C2.

H. G. Twilley Ltd, Roman Mill,
Stamford, Lincs. PE9 1BG.

Yarns
R. J. L. Edwards,
28 Upper East Hayes, Bath BA1 6LP.

USA
Beads
Amar Pearl & Bead Co. Inc.,
19001 Stringway, Long Island City,
New York, 10111.

Glori Bead Shop,
172 West 4th Street, New York,
NY 10012.

Sheru Beads,
49 West 38th Street, New York,
NY 10018.

Notions
John Toggitt Ltd,
52 Vanderbuilt Avenue, New York,
NY 10017.

Threads etc.
American Thread Corporation,
90 Park Avenue, New York, NY 10016.

Bell Yarn Company,
75 Essex Street, New York, NY 10002.

Bucky King Embroideries Unlimited,
121 South Drive, Pittsburgh,
Pennsylvania 15238.

Lily Mills Company,
Shelby, North Carolina, 28150.

Sunray Yarn Company,
349 Grand Street, New York,
NY 10002.

Yarn Bazaar, Yarncrafts Ltd,
3146 M. Street, North West,
Washington D.C. 20007.

Bibliography

Design

Ballinger, Louise Bowen *and*
Vroman, Thomas F. *Design: Sources
and Resources* (Reinhold, 1965).
Comprehensive book which helps the
reader to re-look at his environment.
It is full of inspiration for picture and
pattern making.

de Sausmarez, Maurice. *Basic
Design: The Dynamics of Visual Form*
(Studio Vista, London; Reinhold,
New York, 1964).
Explains simply some of the
elementary principles of basic design,
with useful follow-up exercises.

Rowland, Kurt. *Looking and Seeing*
(Ginn, London, 1969).
Many photographs of patterns,
shapes and textures which could be
used as a basis for your designs.

Embroidery

Butler, Anne *and* Green, David.
Pattern and Embroidery
(Batsford, London; Branford, Mass.
1970).
Shows a creative use of fabrics and
threads and describes many
techniques.

Connor, Margaret. *Introducing
Fabric Collage*
(Watson-Guptill, New York;
Batsford, London, 1969).

Dawson, Barbara. *Metal Thread
Embroidery* (Batsford, London, 1968;
Taplinger, New York, 1969).
An excellent introduction to threads
and their uses.

Dean, Beryl. *Ecclesiastical Embroidery*
(Batsford, London; Branford, Mass.
1968).
A well-illustrated book with much
information that is relevant to other
types of embroidery.

Howard, Constance. *Inspiration for
Embroidery* (Batsford, London;
Branford, Mass. 1967).
A well-illustrated book which lives
up to its title.

John, Edith. *Creative Stitches*
(Batsford, London; Branford, Mass.
1967).
A standard stitch book for all
needleworkers.

Jones, Mary Eirwen. *A History of
Western Embroidery* (Studio Vista,
London; Watson-Guptill, New York,
1969).

Krevitsky, Nik. *Stitchery: Art and
Craft* (Van Nostrand-Reinhold,
New York, 1966).

Schuette, Marie *and* Christensen,
Sigrid Muller. *The Art of Embroidery*
(Thames and Hudson, 1964).
This and Jones are two helpful books
on the history of embroidery.

*Mary Thomas's Dictionary of
Embroidery Stitches* (Hodder &
Stoughton, London, 1954).
A dictionary which gives detailed
descriptions, with diagrams, of a
large number of stitches and their
uses.

Mary Thomas's Embroidery Book
(Hodder & Stoughton, London, 1953).
Describes in detail many classic
forms of embroidery.

Wilson, Erica. *Crewel Embroidery.*
(Charles Scribner's Sons, New York,
1962).

100 Stitches (Coats/Anchor)
A small but very useful book with
excellent stitch diagrams.

Knotting and Cording. Dryad Leaflet
No. 127.
Gives instruction in making cords
which are suitable for use as threads.

Tie and Dye with Dylon. A Dylon
pamphlet.
This explains how to dye and tie dye
fabrics. Simple recipes are included.

Periodicals

Crafts. Published bi-monthly by
the Crafts Advisory Committee,
28 Haymarket, London SW1Y 4SU.
A magazine for the craftsman and
all those interested in his work.

Craft Horizons. Published bi-monthly
by the American Craftsmens Council,
44 West 53rd Street, New York 19.
Publishes articles on the whole field
of crafts, past and present, but its
coverage of the contemporary scene
is very good.

Graphis. Published bi-monthly by
Walter Herdeg, Graphis Press,
Zurich, Switzerland.
A sparkling, up to the minute
magazine, full of excellent examples
of modern design in many fields.